AF255959

WHEN GRANDMOTHER SPEAKS

WHEN GRANDMOTHER SPEAKS

poems
from an
animal
communicator

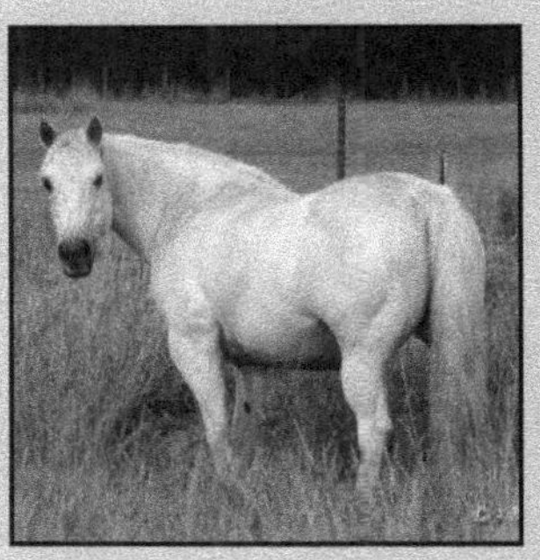

DONNA SAUER

PHOTOGRAPHS BY J. BELLE PHOTOGRAPHY

Published by Mystique of Animals Publications
For more information, visit www.drdonnaac.com

Book design by Constellation Book Services,
www.constellationbookservices.com

ISBN (hardcover): 978-0-578-33381-6

Printed in the United States of America

To all who taught me.

WHEN GRANDMOTHER SPEAKS

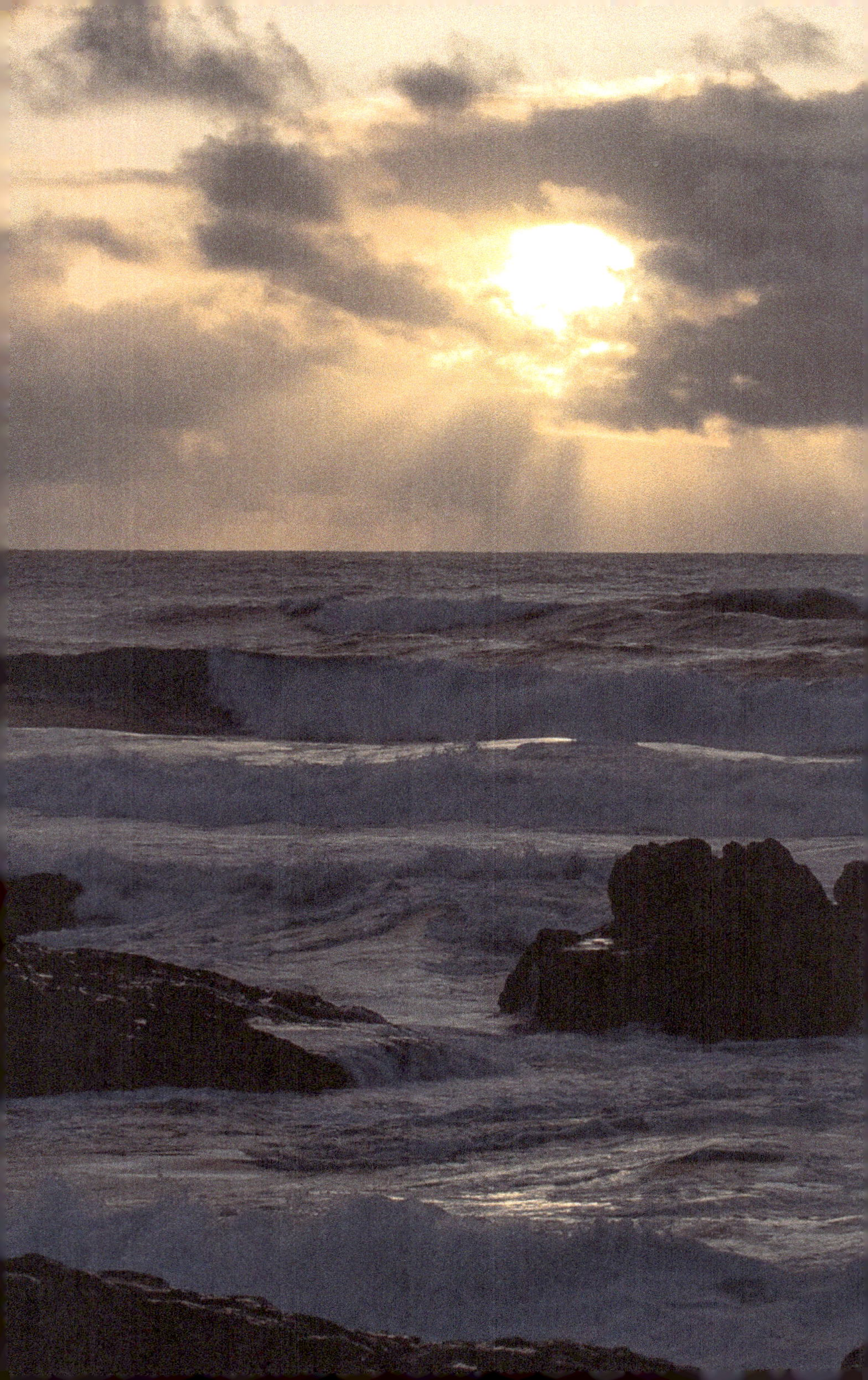

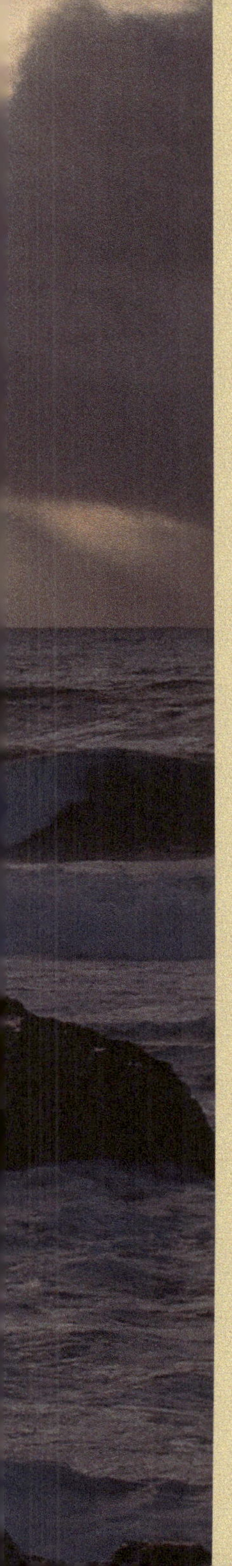

The oceans widen up,
the earth rolls
and laughs…

The gulls caw,
the crows cry….

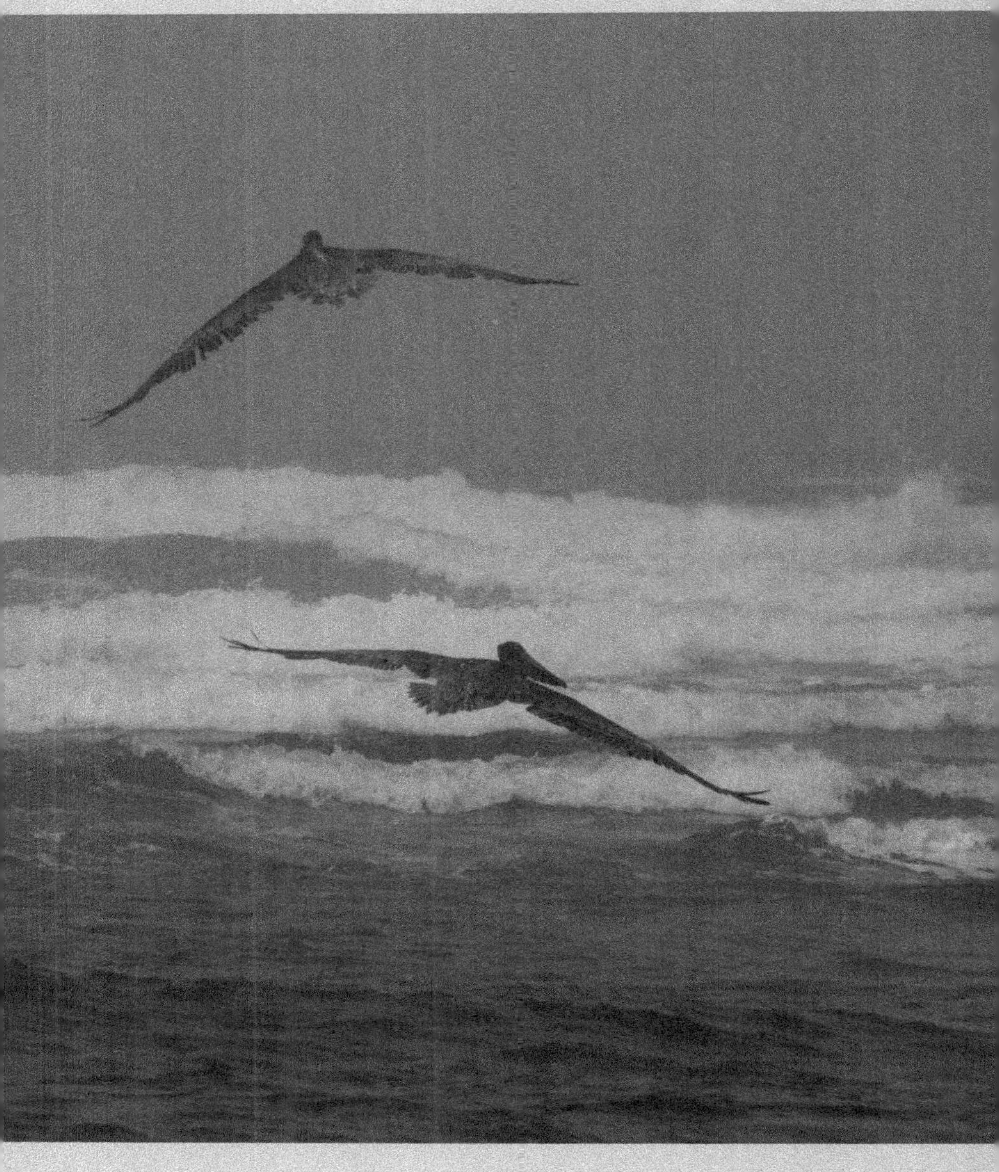

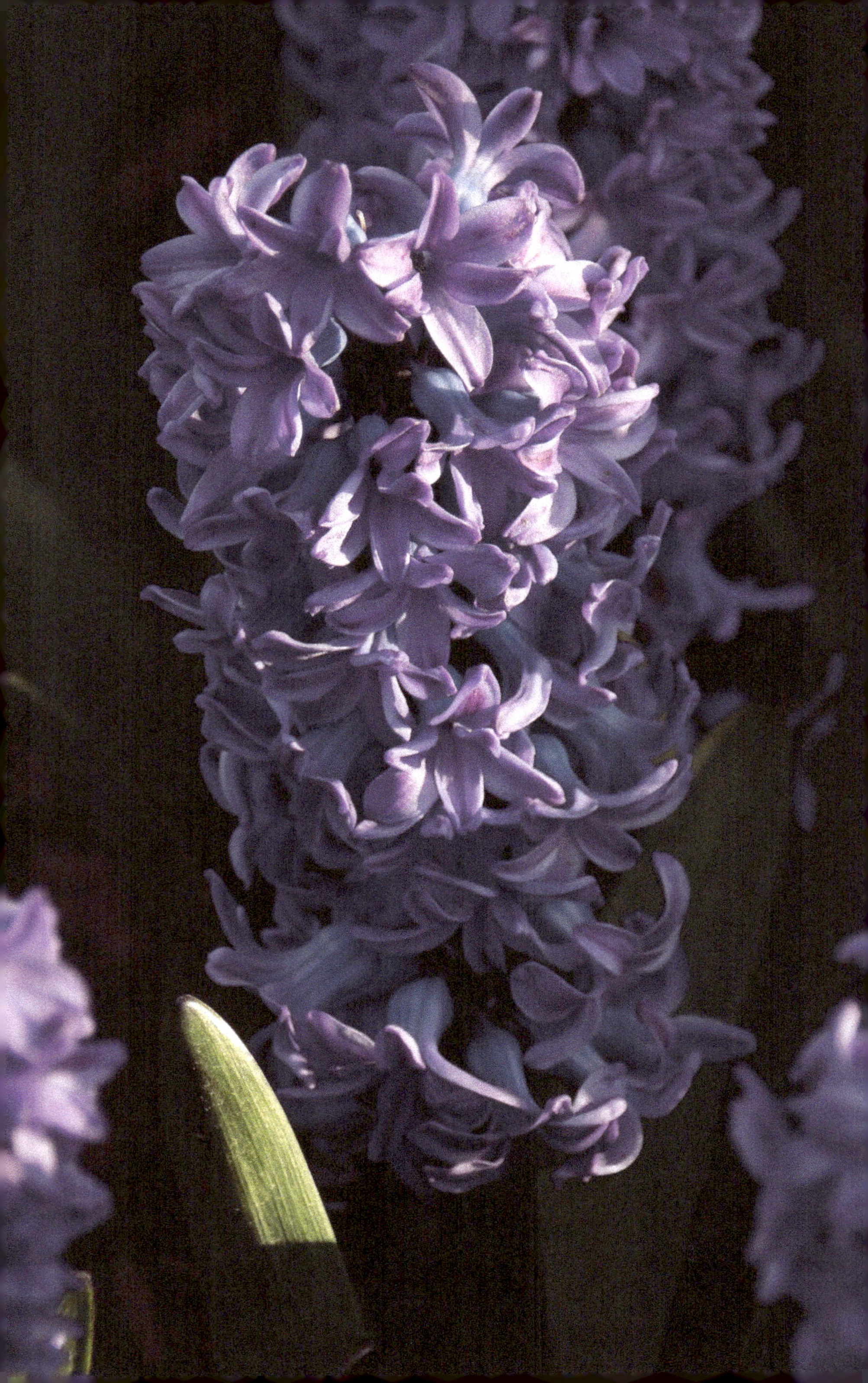

The sun shines,
the irises bend
and bob their heads…

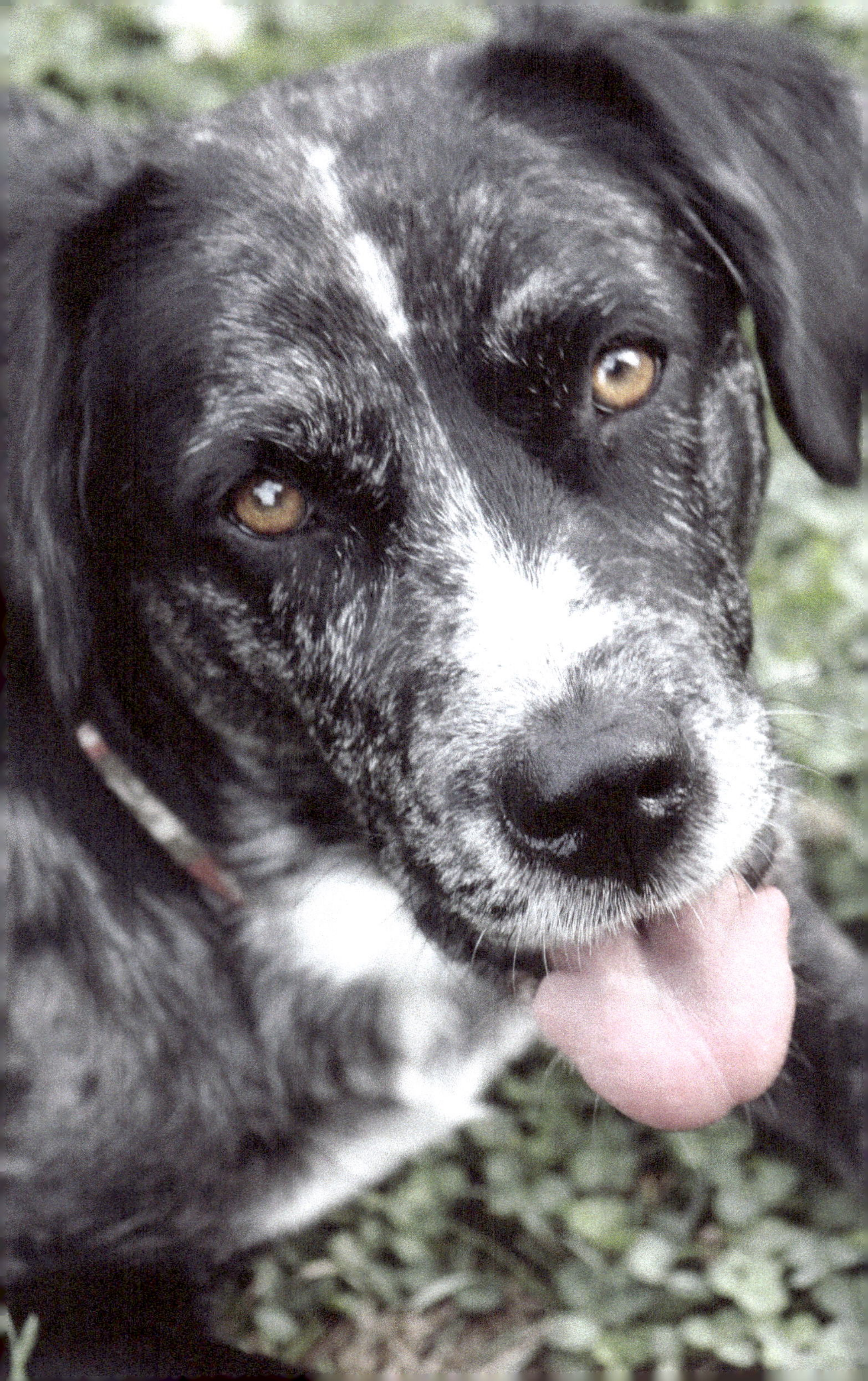

The dogs howl,
the birds hop up
and down…

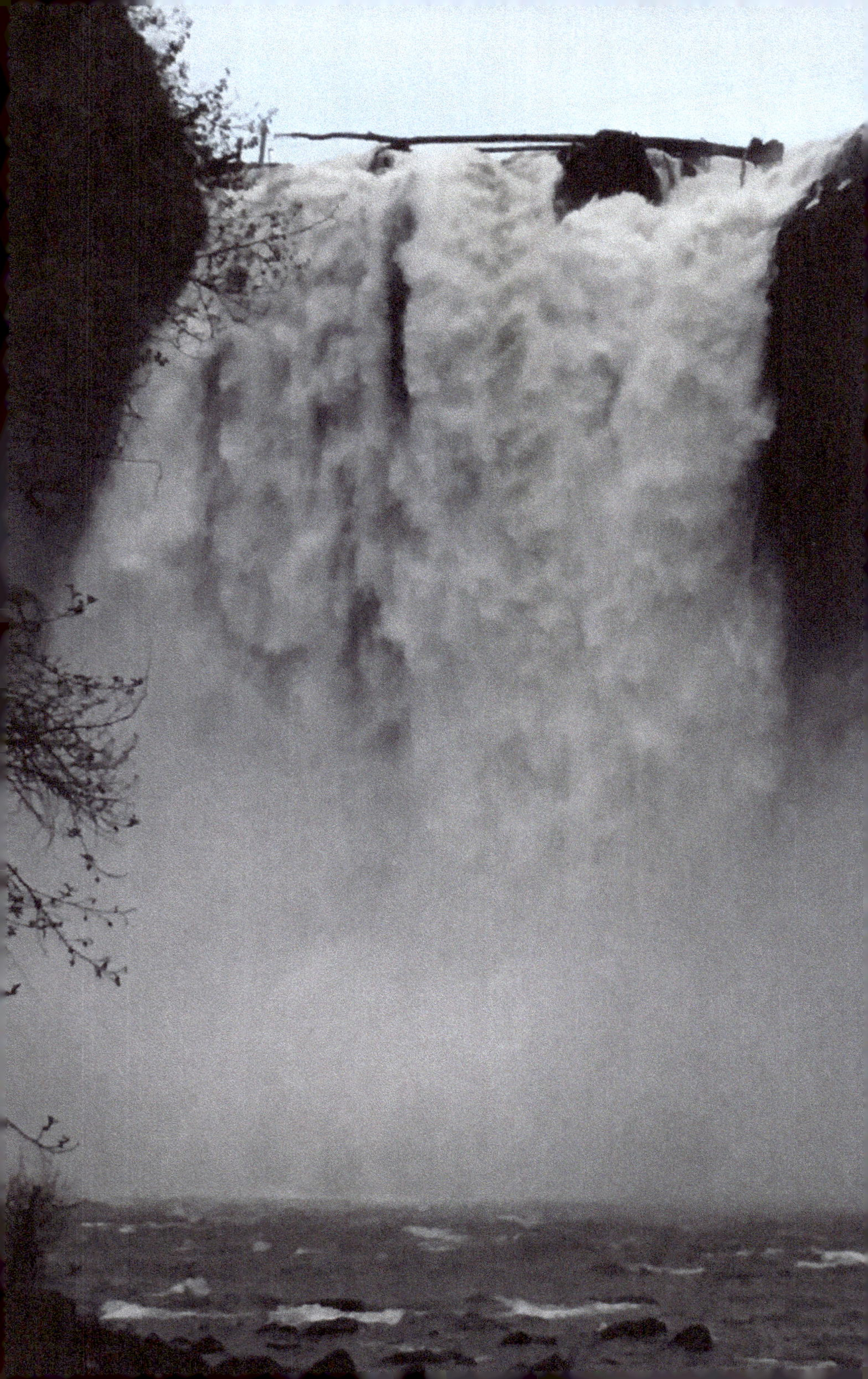

The drainage ditches
flow, the water rises…

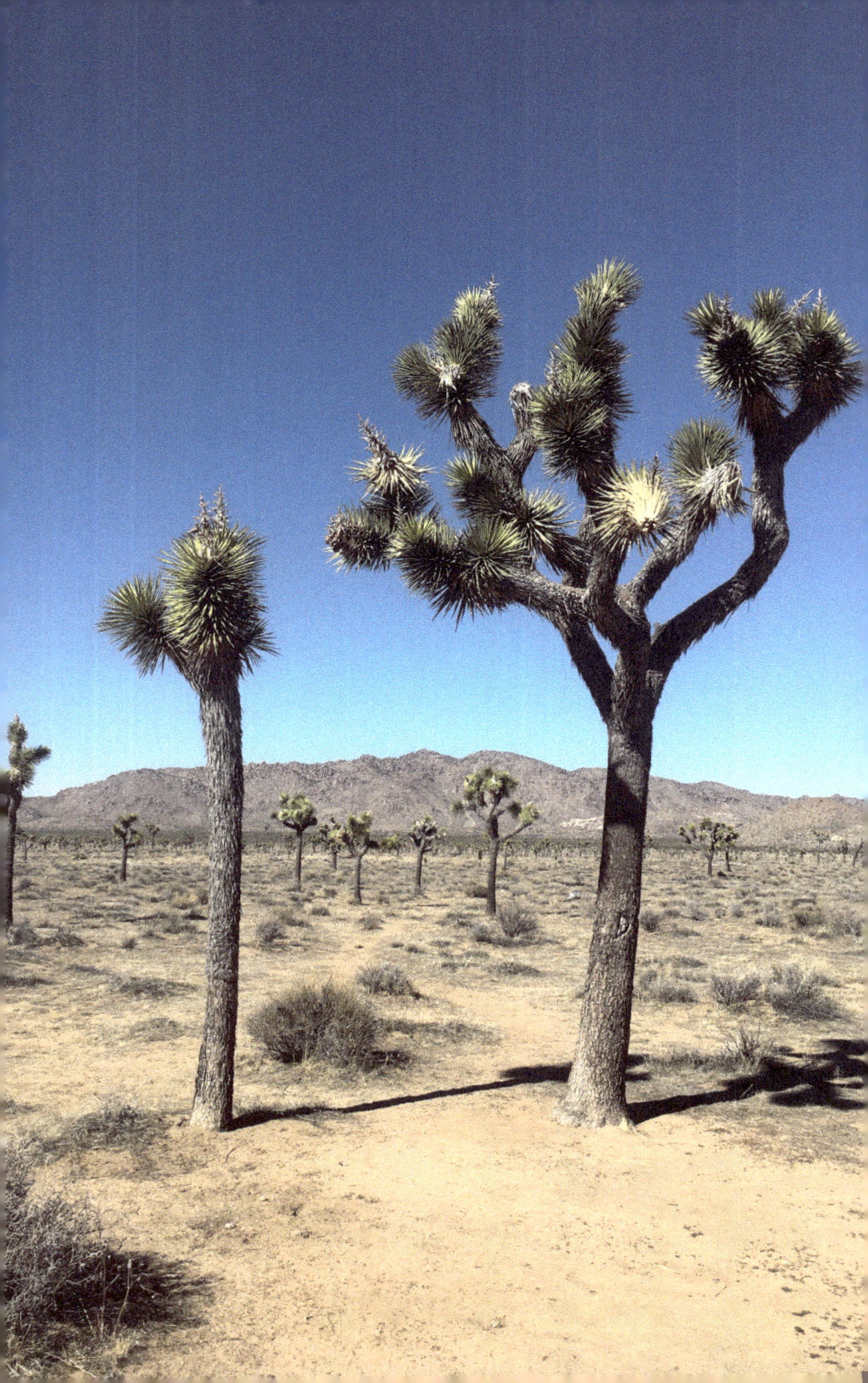

The floods come and overflow, the parched plains drink…

The stars twinkle,
the ants sing praise…

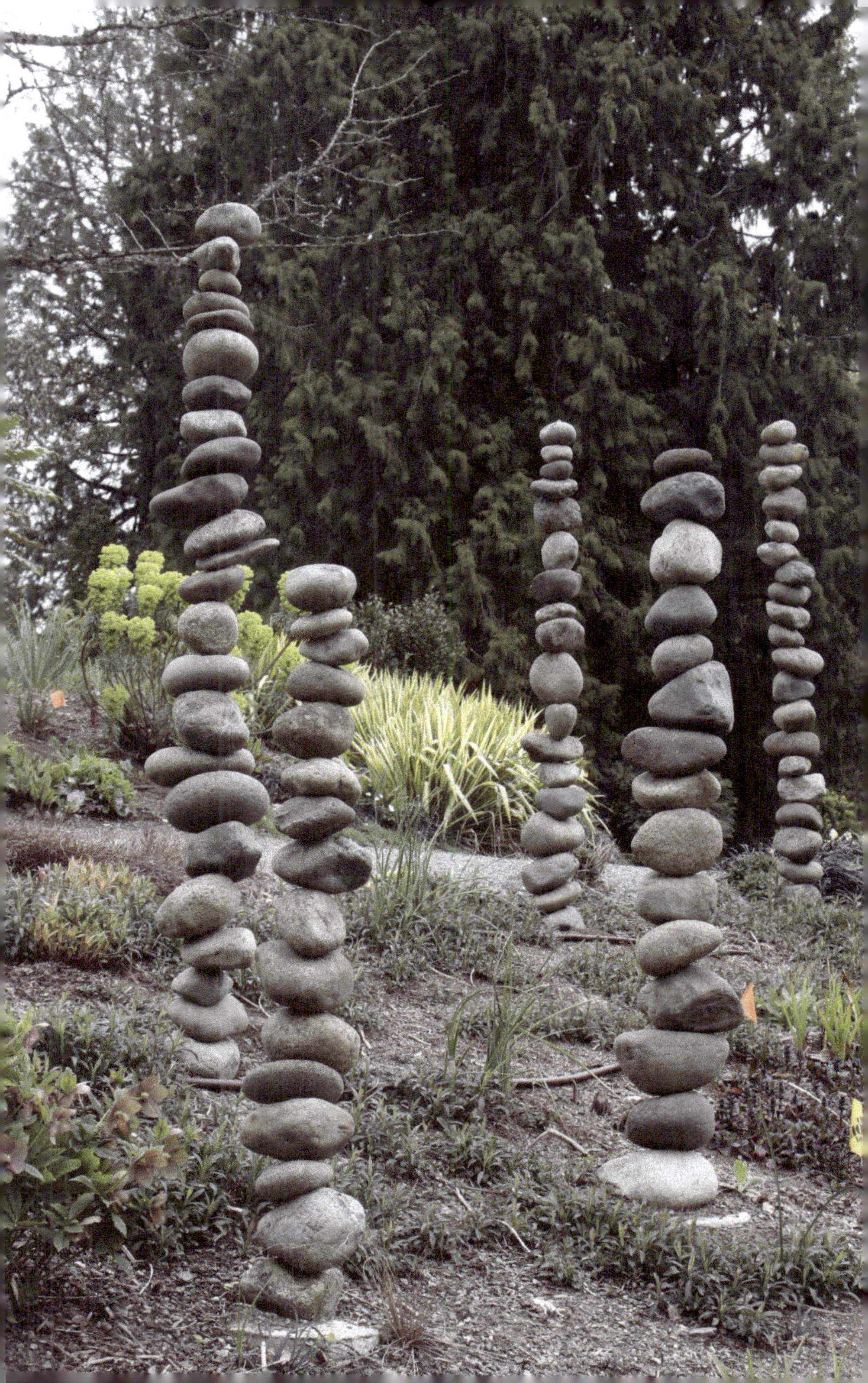

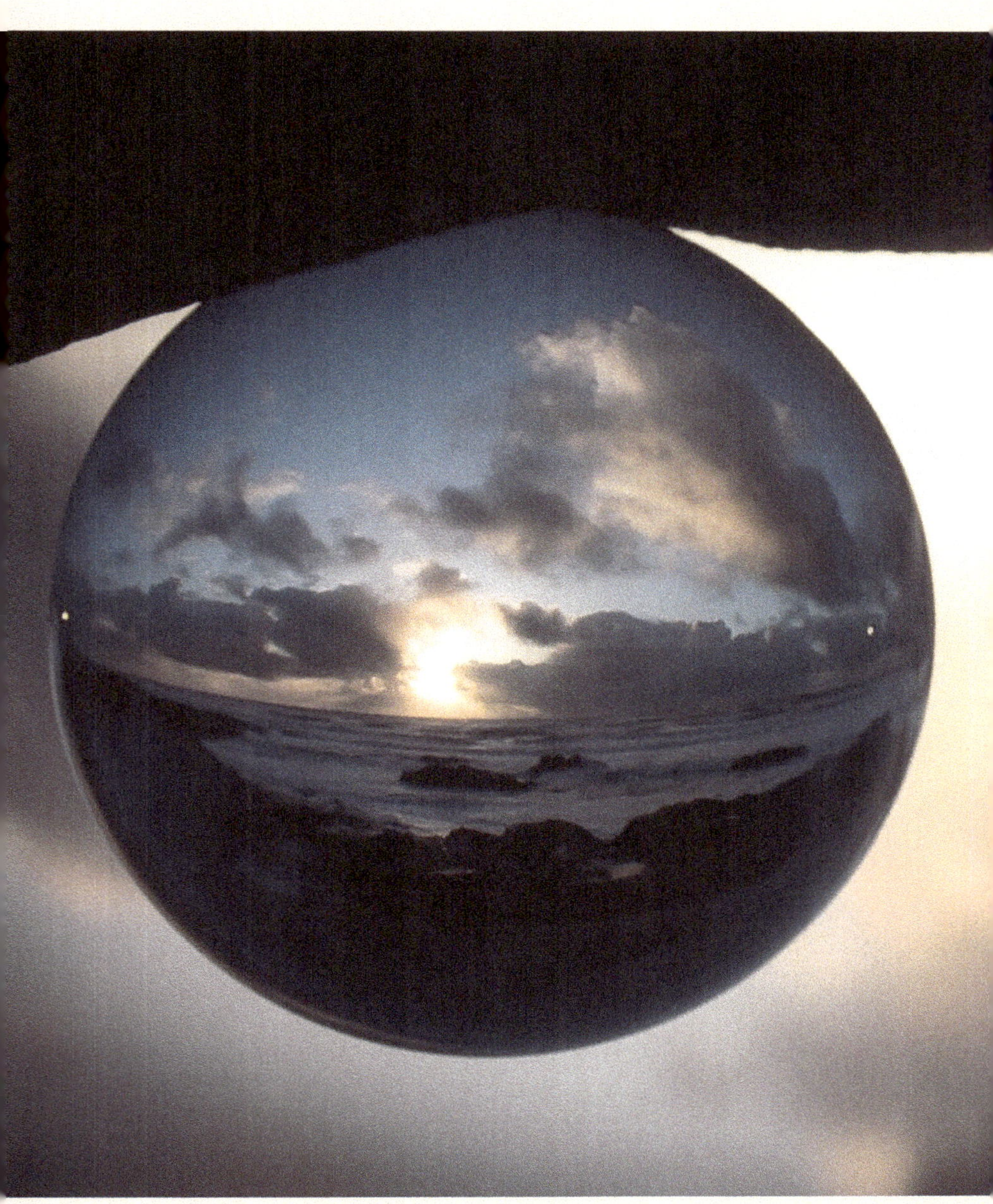

The earth turns
and turns again…

The heavens roar,
great craters form….

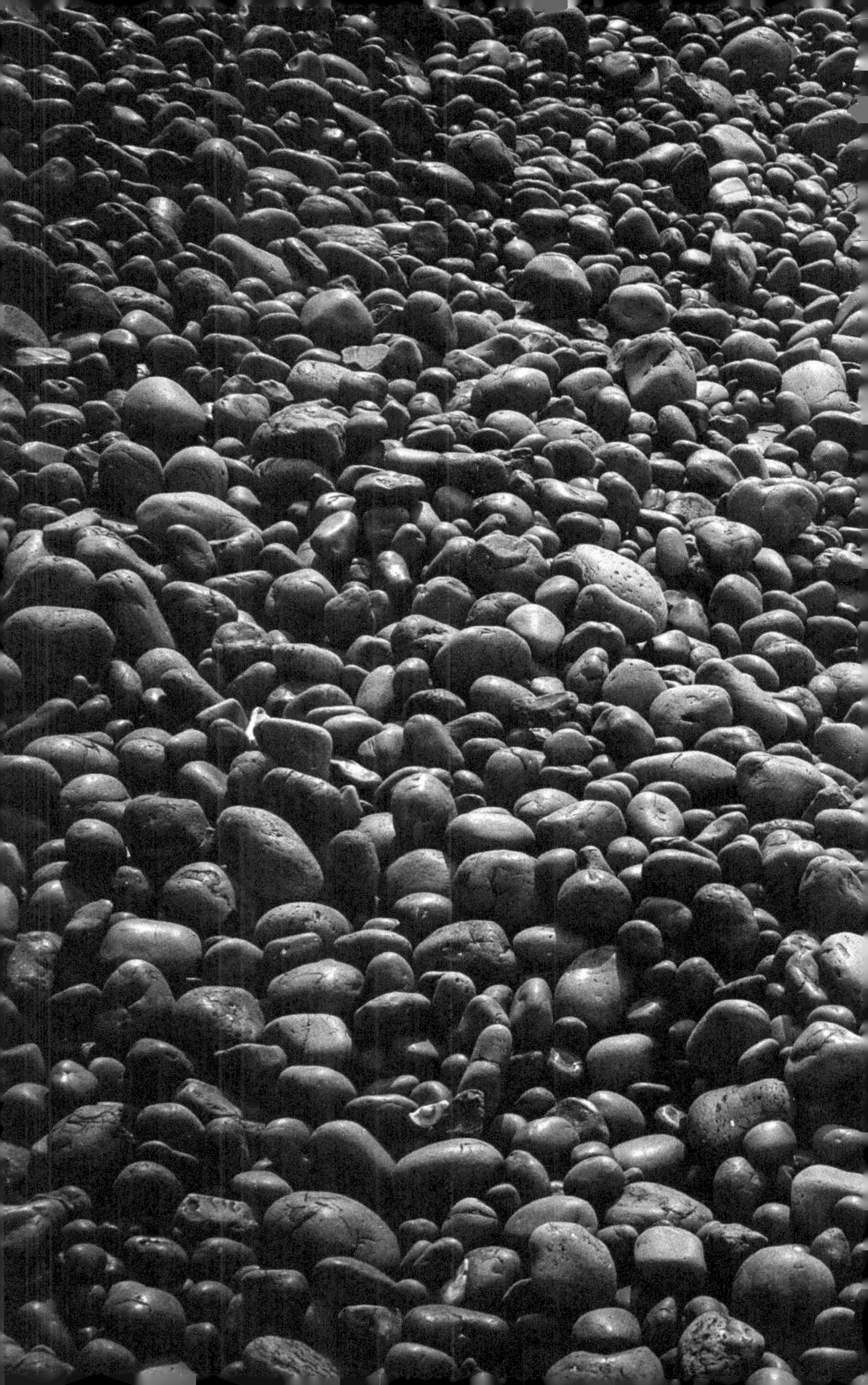

Meteors rush by
as the hair on the
dogs bristles with
anticipation…

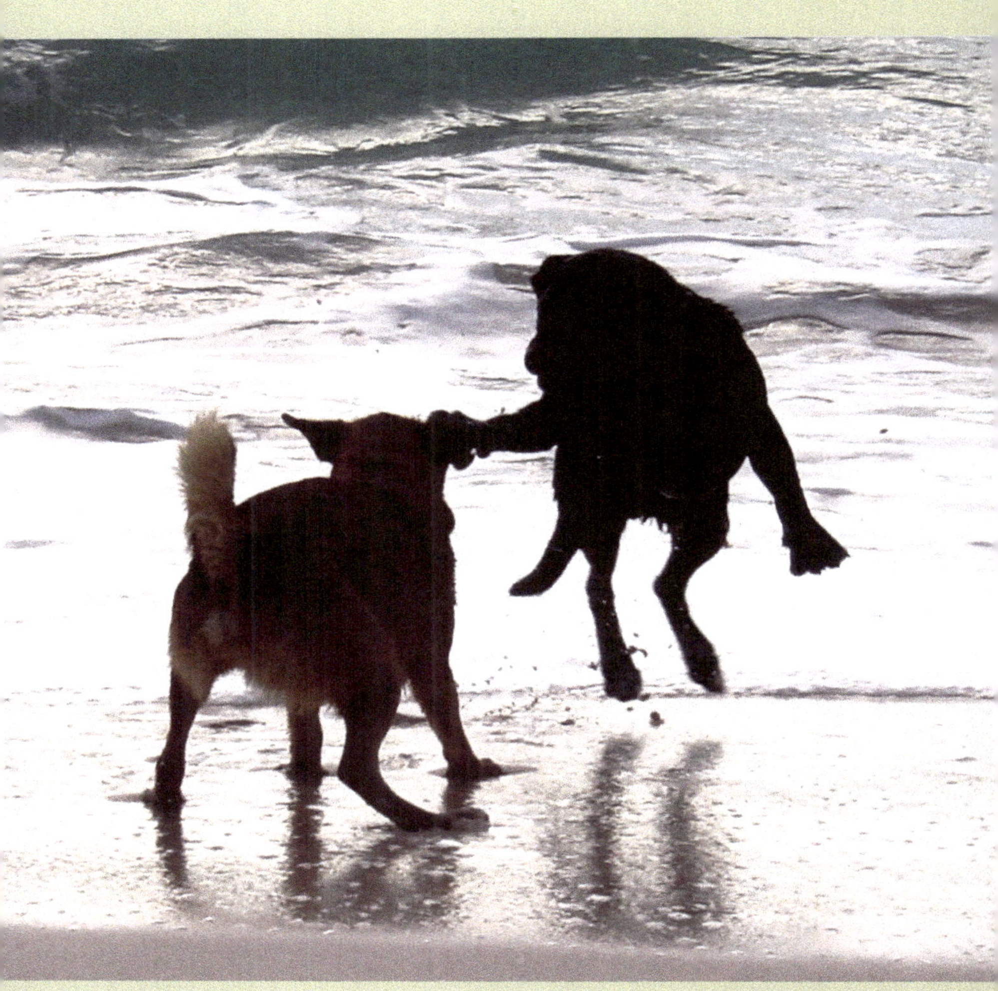

The moon rises and
sighs, and drips a
few tears..

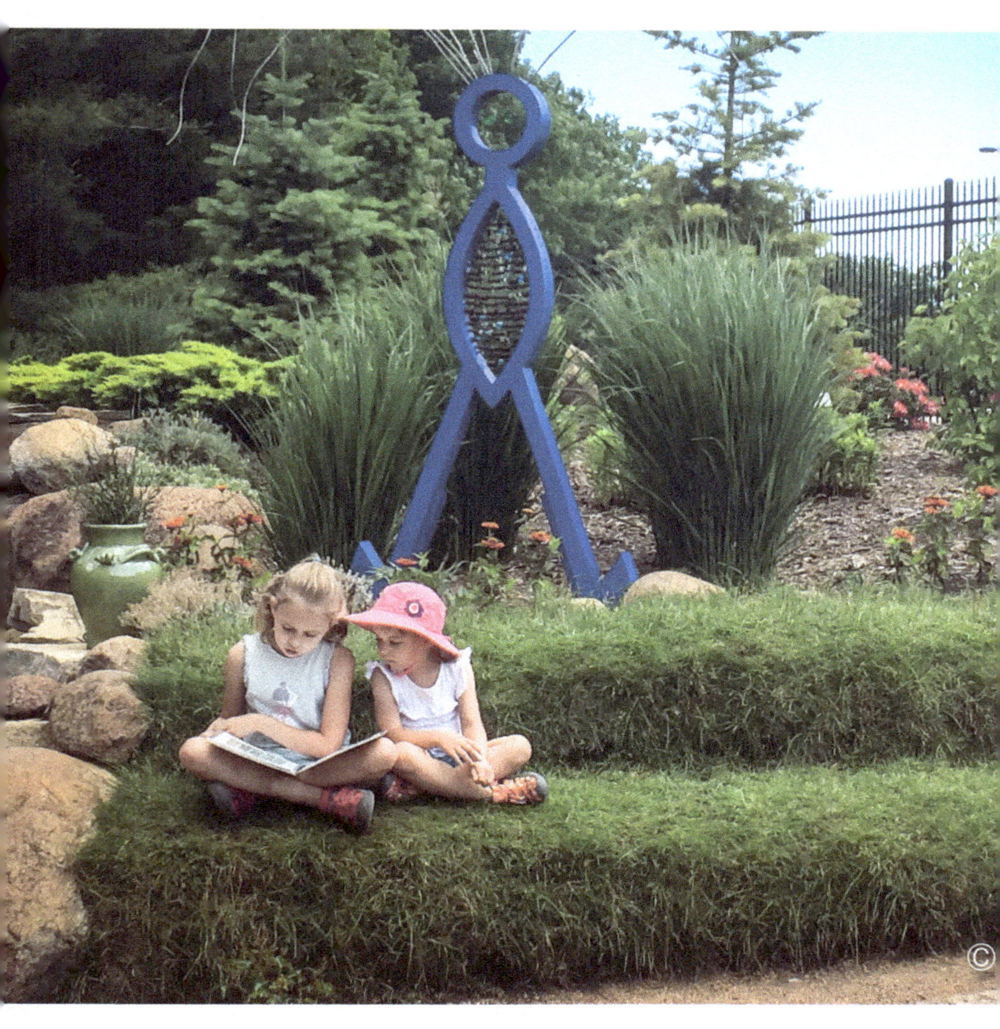

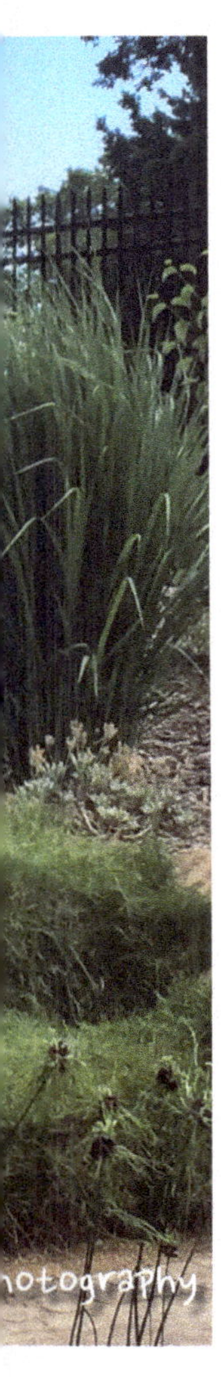

The children laugh,
the daughter loves
the mother unendingly…

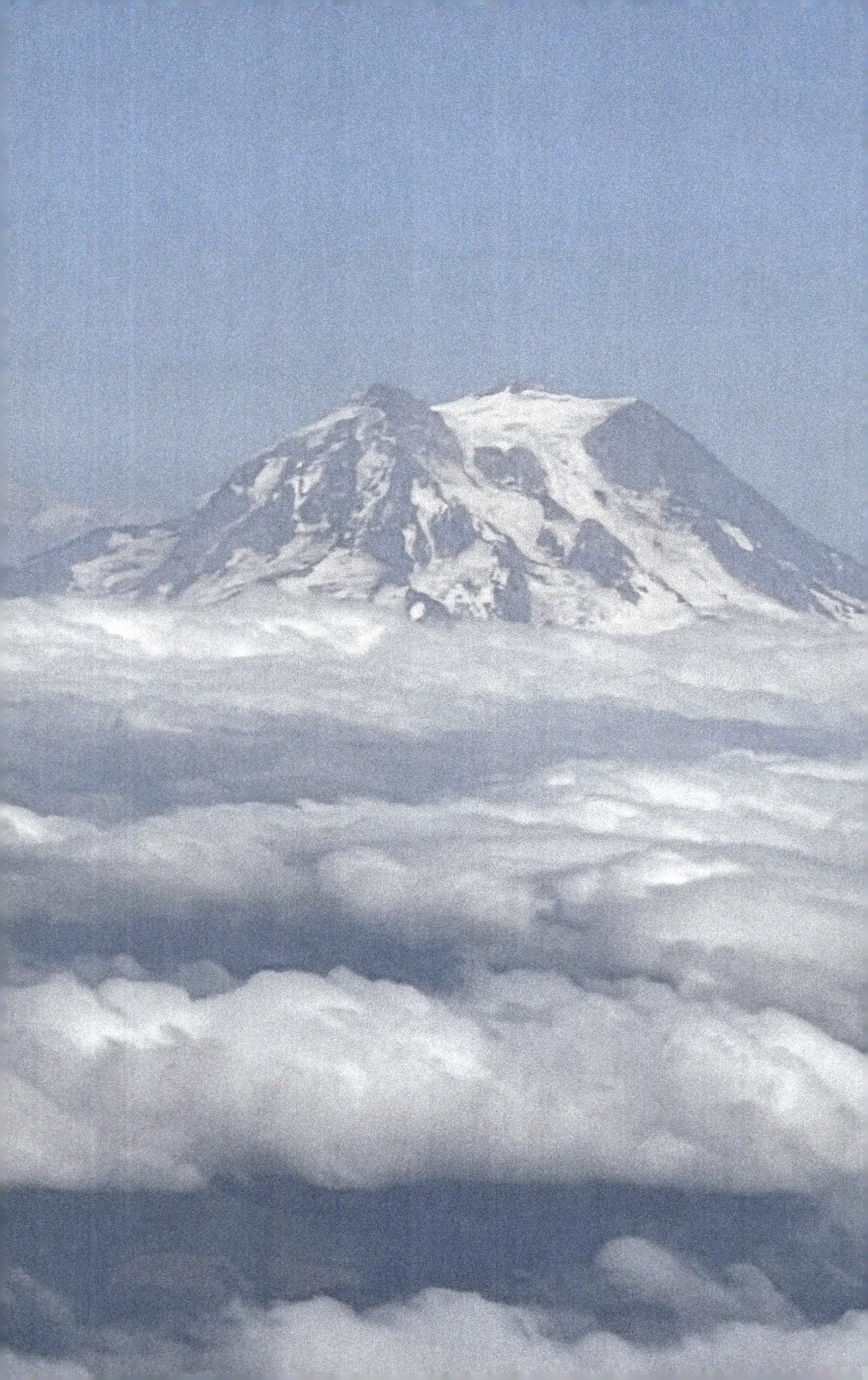

The earth moves and
shudders and shakes,
great mountains arise
from the seas….

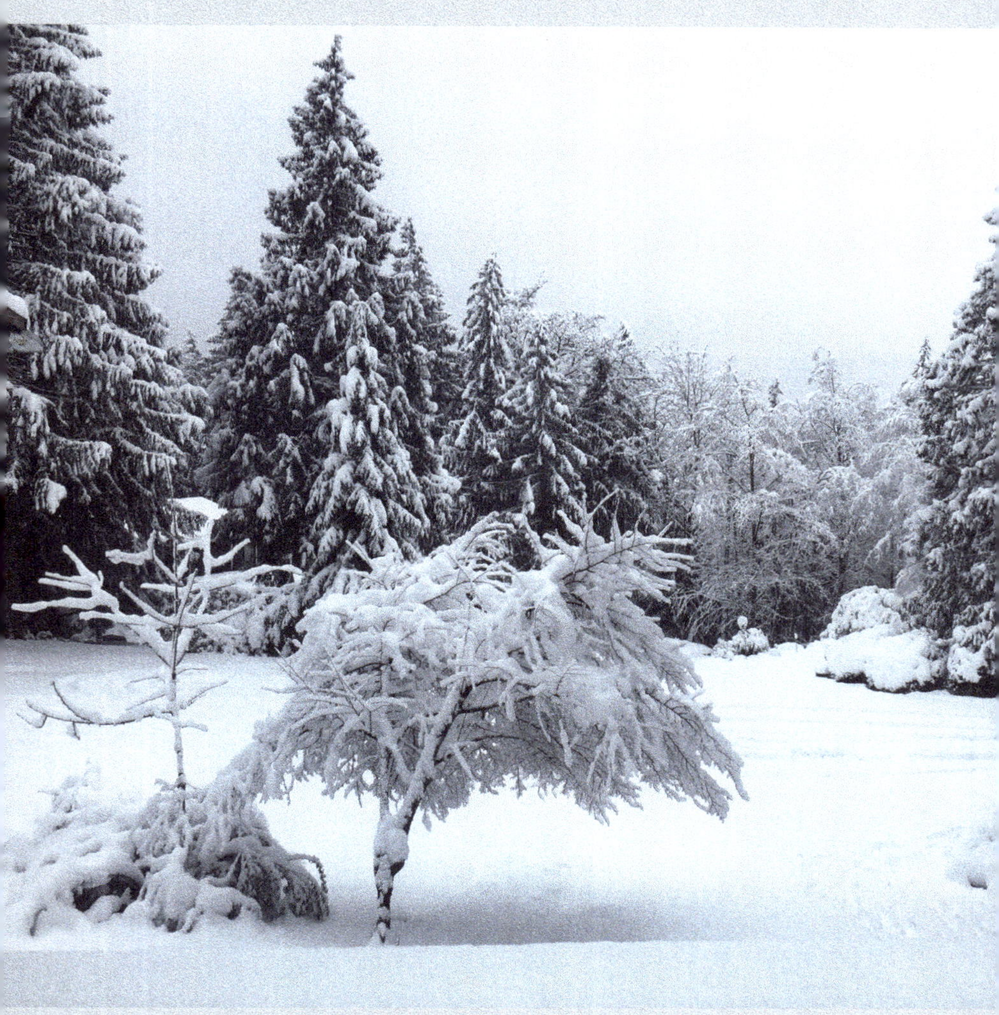

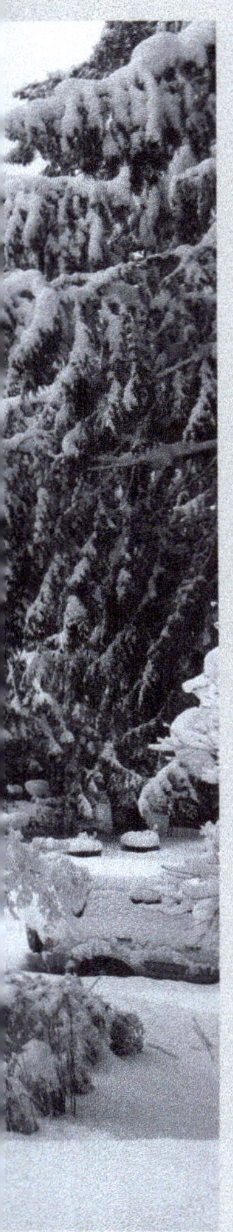

The heavens send their gases to coalesce and sparkle like diamonds…

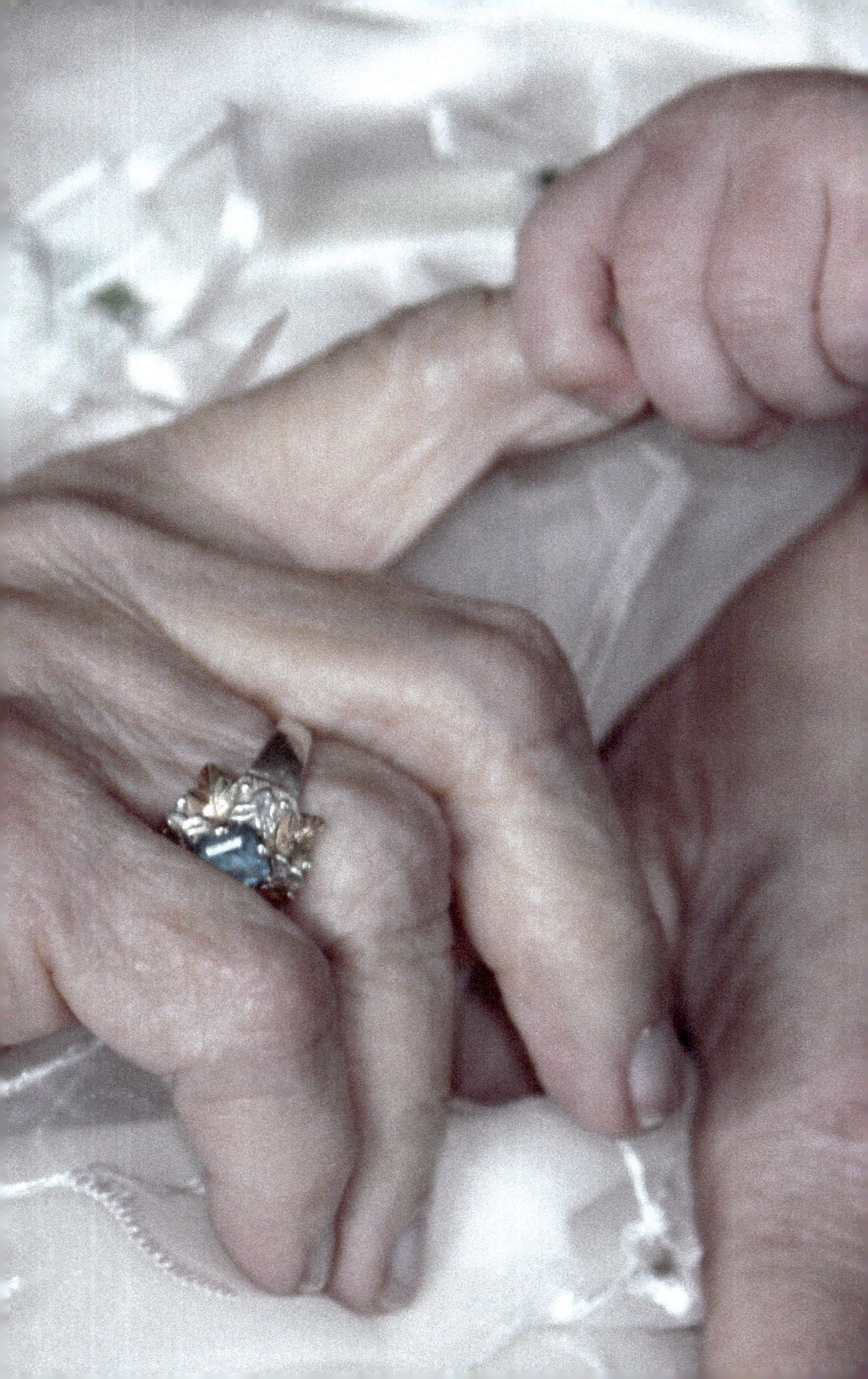

Love comes…

Pink clouds
of comfort
surround
and hug,
and love
infinitesimally…..

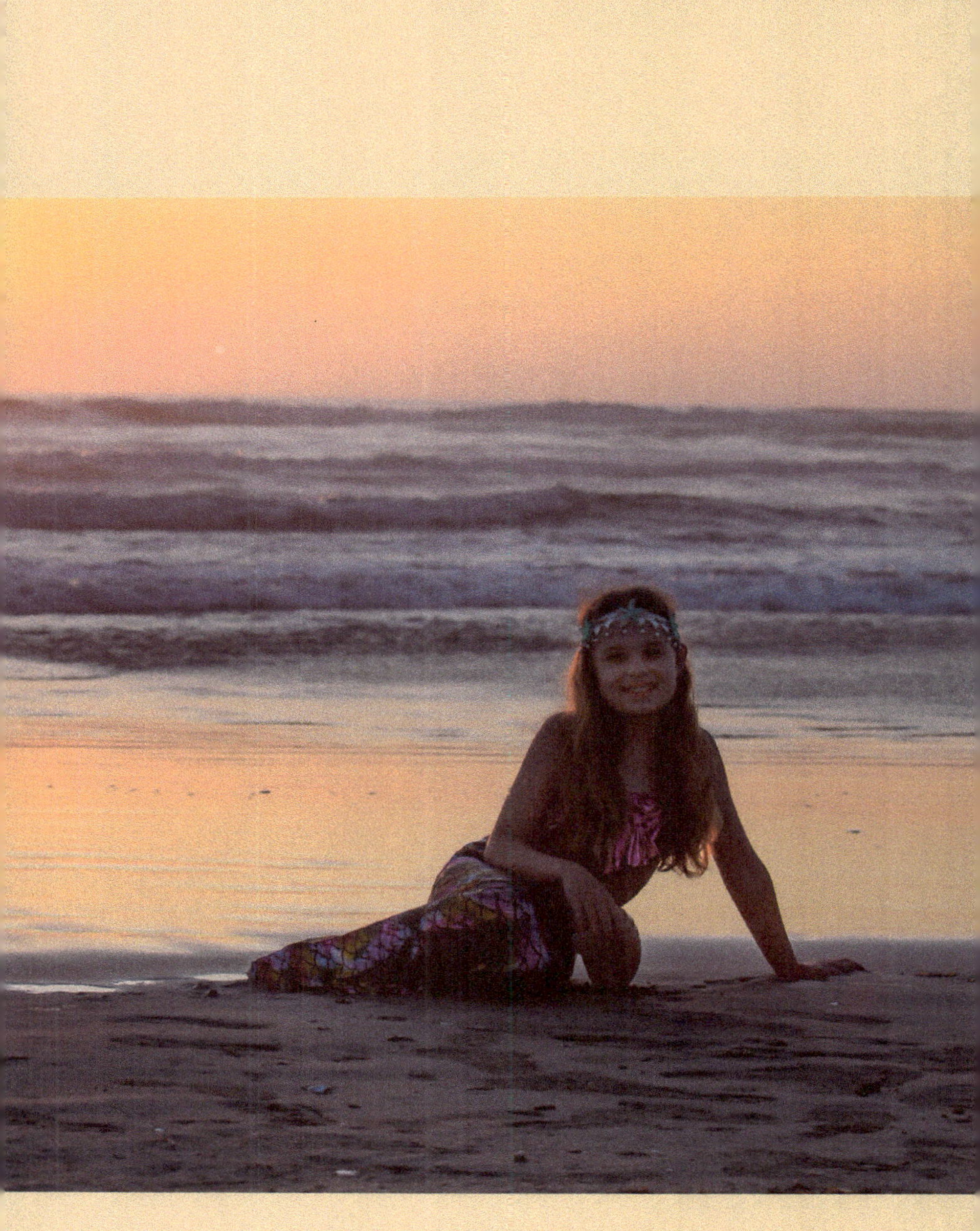

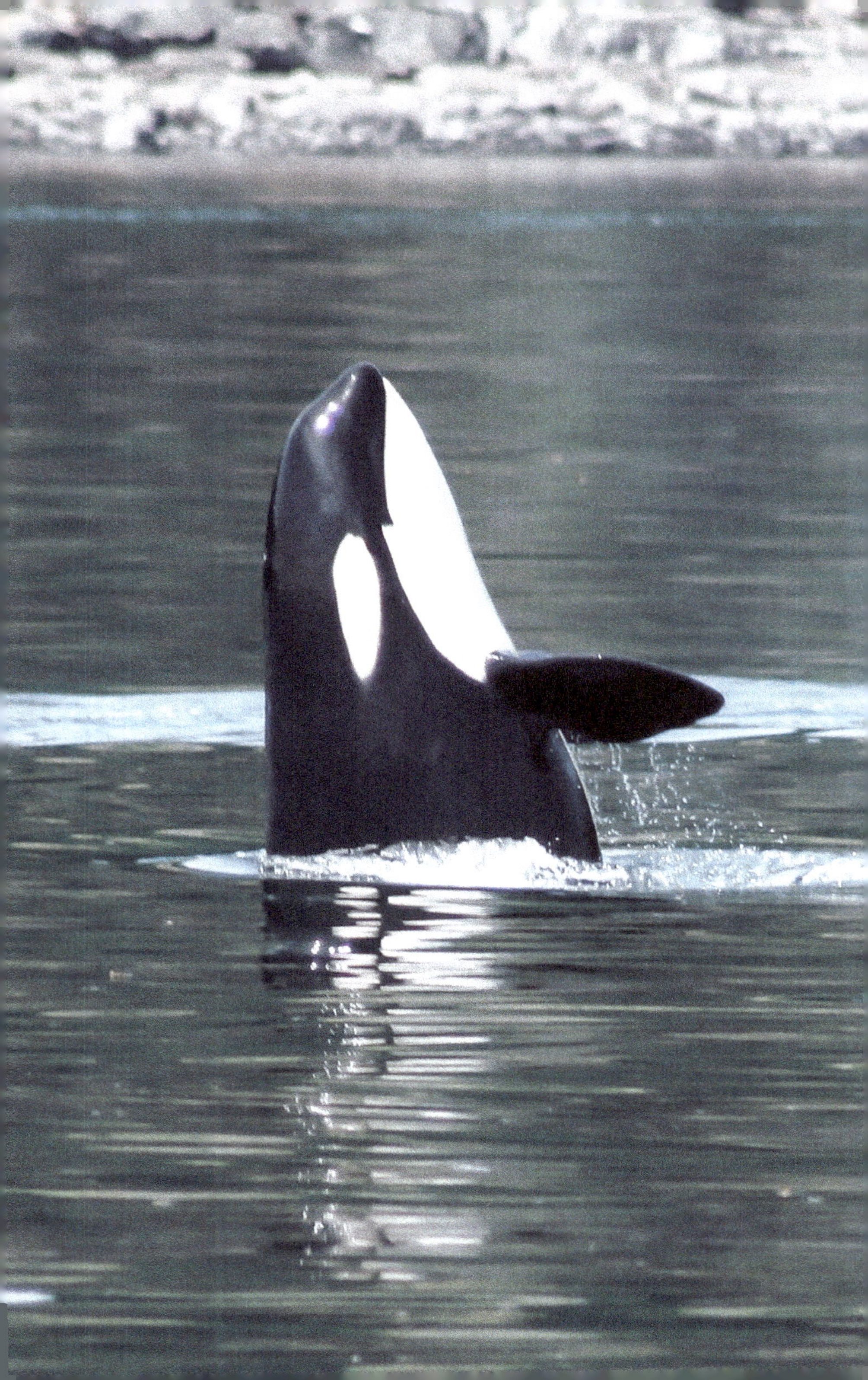

All of creation vibrates
with love when
Grandmother speaks…

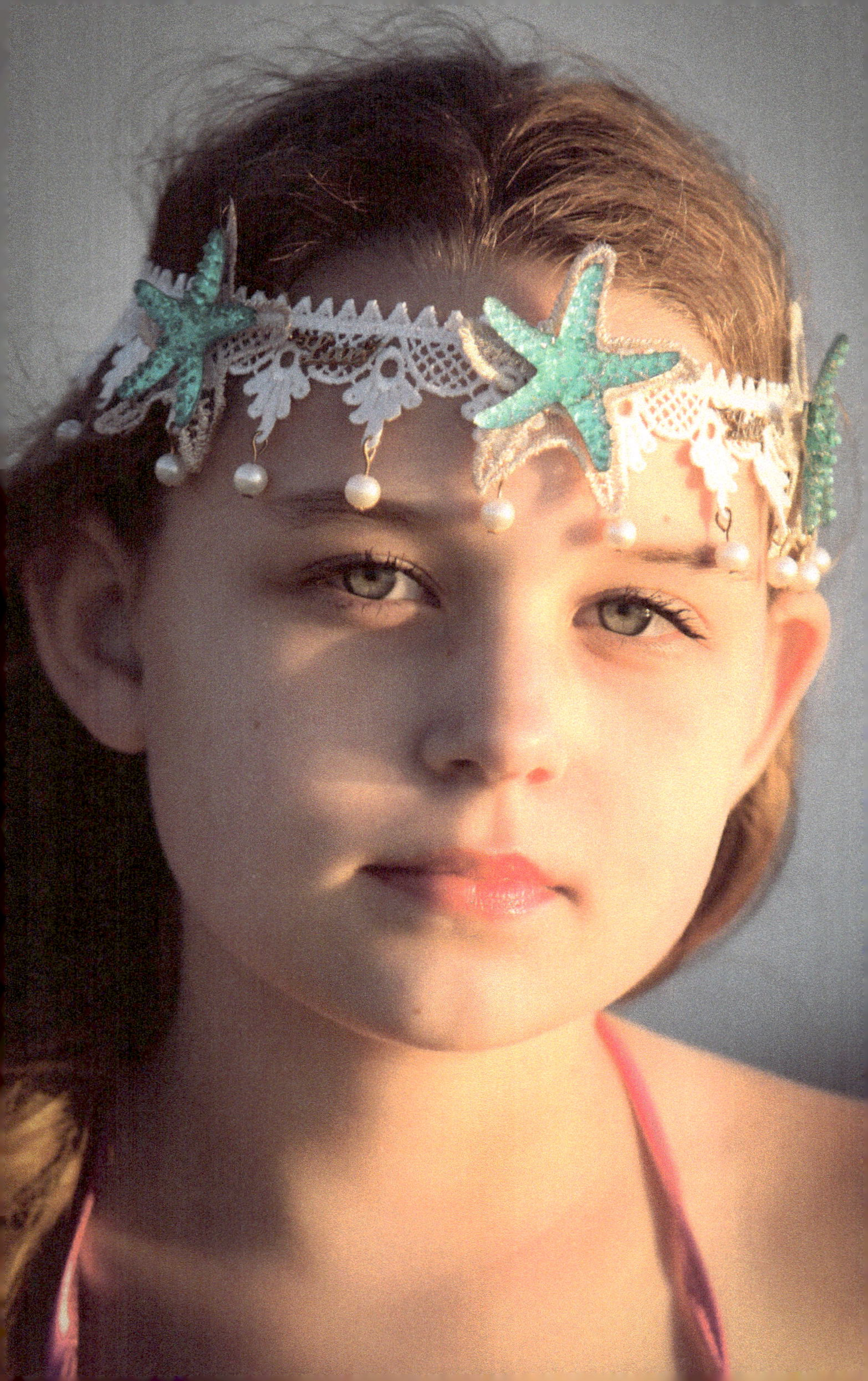

PEACE

Peace is all at once, all encompassing.
    All for all—within all, without all.

Peace is eternal. Peace is love. It is quiet,
    non-turbulent, soothing, loving, giving, growing,
    blooming, life, death,
    all forever.

Live Peace. Live your peace, give
    your peace to all around you.

Grow in health and wealth with your peace. Peace is all
    you want, all you need to follow your blessed path.

Pray. Send healing energy to all who need peace, who
    need the grace of peace, who need the quiet,
    gentle murmur of peace within themselves.

Peace generates peace, radiates out through love,
    warmth, knowing, accepting,
    understanding.

Peace flows like yellow honey, the love of light, the
    eternal knowledge of all that is.

Live in peace.

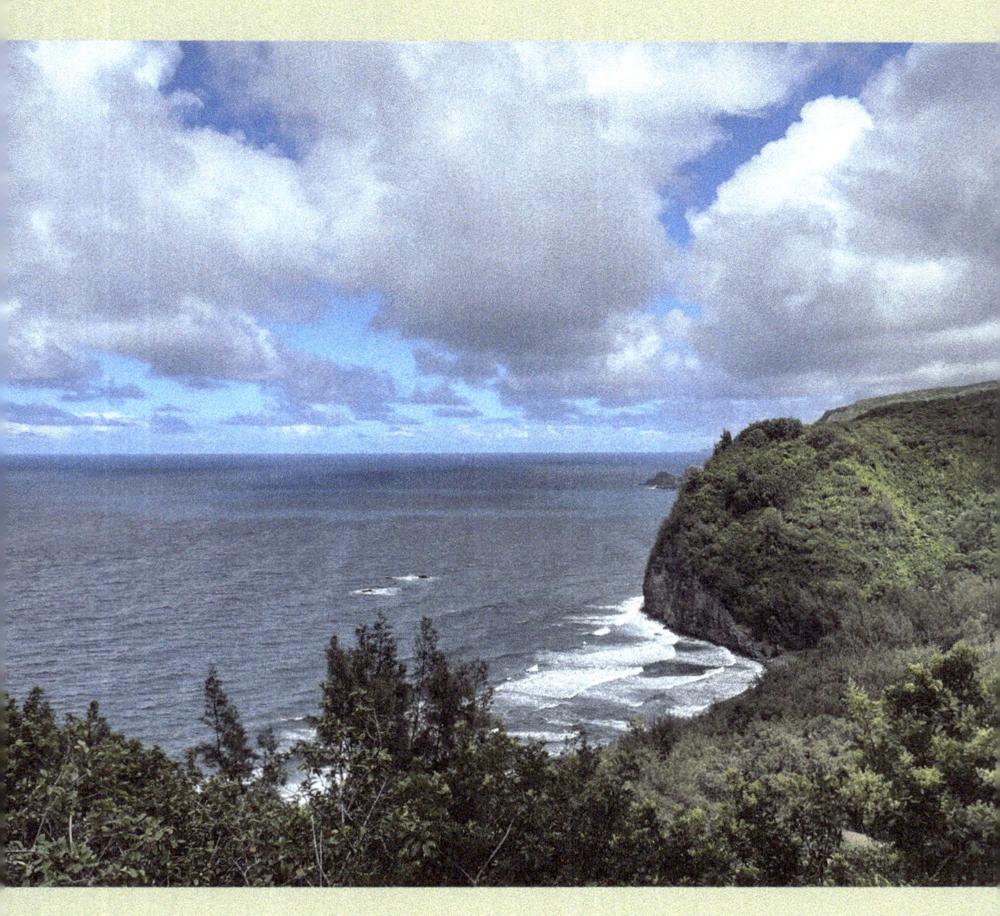

LISTENING

Listen to the leaves—
    Hear their rustle, their rhythm,
        the never-ending song of love and living.

Listen to the grass—
    Loving your feet on itself,
        joyous to be green and living.
    Hear the earth,
        the very blessed whispering of the ground itself.

Listen to the wind—
    The safety of the brushing of the boughs in the trees.
    Listen closely as the wind blows in little breezes, the warmth of the
        air on you,
        so happy to be caressing your face,
        waking you to possibilities, keeping you active and happy.

Listen to the water—
    Gurgling, gleeful, moving, transforming, shapeless,
        making waves and furrows and ripples,
        forever and by ever lasting and being.
    Hear the ancient siren song,
        that old beauty of the deep soul of longing and caring,
        which even the depth of the ocean does not reach.

Listen to the distant drums—
    Feel the dance, the SunDance, and be one with them.
    Support them and reverberate with them.
    They are Grandmother's heart beat.
    Remember this always and bring the rhythm into your being.

Listen to the footsteps upon Grandmother's hair—
    Ahead, beside, behind you.
    They are the energy of millennia of years, times, galaxies.
    These good souls follow you, lead you, walk beside you,
        in all manners of being.
    Walk peacefully and quietly with them in the bridging grace.

Listen to the air—
    In absolute quietness it brings peace.

Listen—
    You are one with them all.

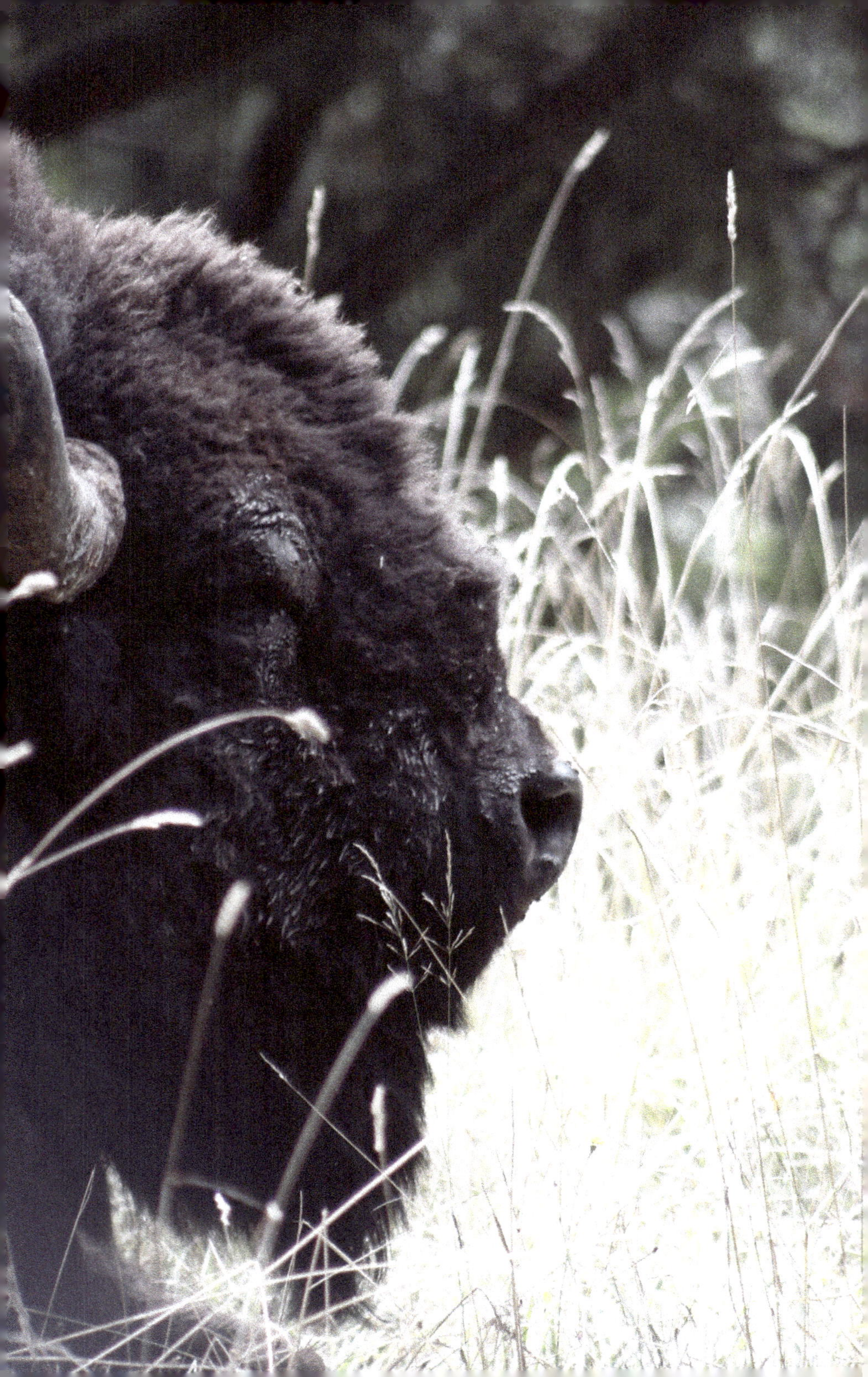

KNOWING

Be guided to the strength and assuredness of knowing—

Knowing is as you perceive it—
    loving and protective, swirling with the energy of love from all that
    has gone before.

The experiences are in your fabric—
    but only serve to sew the threads of your new coat, your new
    hatchling, always emerging spirit.

There is no past, no present, no future—
    There is just "IS," the reality of existence, no more, no less,
    encompassing every being, every breath, every energy, rumbling,
    wave, breeze, utterance.

Come be with with us this day—
    Dwell in the comfort of melding with the "IS."
    You are so important, so needed, so respected, so loved.

Your "footprint" resonances with "IS"—
    with Grandmother Earth, with all the Star Nation and ancestors.

Like the siren call of the mermaids, you attract the most loving of souls,
    the most beauteous of
    beings, the most quiet and serene.

Continue to heal and help others—
    It is your life now—everything. Help all who seek you as you
    are yourself protected and loved.

    Do you see the smoothing of the waves, the quieting of the
    gale winds, the hushing of sound, the simmering of the great
    fire, the slowing of the Buffalo hooves?

All comes into rhythm as the energies work together—
New levels of vibrations are reached. Take in what you need, send
out the rest to those in need of comfort and love and
healing and balancing.

Be grateful for your path—
It is all of the above and more.

You will return to us whole, mended, grown to fruition, expanded, full
of the universe of the All, " the "IS."

About the Author

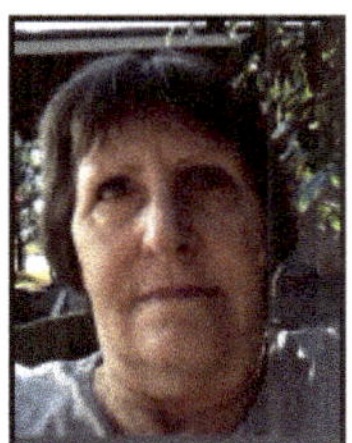

Dr. Donna Sauer has a master's degree in Zoology as well as a PhD in biology. After many years of teaching sciences at the college level, she now directs her life work towards Animal Communication and Energy Healing. She is a graduate of the Lynn McKenzie Animal Energy Communication Institute and also a Reiki Master and follower of Lakota Healing Traditions.

She resides in Washington State on a small farm which she shares with rescue animals and a plethora of trees and flowers, all of which delight, teach and energize her each and every day.

Her animal communication readings and energy healing session keep her busy along with writings and teaching animal communication skills. At the heart of her work is a wish to help each unique being come into the full potential of their divine life path within the universality of unconditional love and acceptance.

Contact information:

Dr. Donna Sauer
Animal Energy Healer and Communicator
www.drdonnaac.com

J. Belle Photography
www.pixbyjenn.zenfolio.com